The Power of Beauty

Unmasking Its History

and Impact

Sarah Davis

Preface

The Power of Beauty Unmasking Its History and Impact

For thousands of years, people have been fascinated by the idea of beauty, which has the power to alter people's perspectives and affect many aspects of daily life. This book explores the timeless tradition of beauty, following its inception from the reflections of classical philosophers to its diverse function in contemporary culture.

Although opinions on beauty change throughout time, the book investigates whether there are some qualities that could be considered universally attractive by people from different cultural backgrounds. The book examines the biological foundations of our ability to choose between attractive and repulsive appearances using ideas such as facial averageness, symmetry, and sexual dimorphism.

We look at the timeless impact of youth on face attractiveness, emphasizing how it has always been there throughout history. But the book goes beyond a single definition of beauty, recognizing the enormous influence of one's surroundings and experiences in forming one's own viewpoints.

Additionally, the book explores the different and changing standards of beauty among White, Asian, Black, and Latino cultures, delving into the complexity of race and ethnicity. The book then looks at how globalization has affected society as a whole, discussing how it has challenged cultural norms and spread foreign beauty standards.

In the end, this book reveals the complex relationship between beauty and its individual, cultural, and historical components. It encourages a deeper comprehension of this potent and dynamic idea by inviting readers to go on an exploratory trip.

Acknowledgments:

I want to express my gratitude to everyone who supported me throughout the journey of writing this book. To my friends and family, thank you for your unwavering encouragement and understanding during the long hours spent at my desk. Your belief in me kept me going, even when the words seemed to escape me.

I'm incredibly thankful for the guidance and expertise of those who helped shape this project into what it is today. Whether it was offering insights, conducting research, or providing feedback, your contributions were invaluable.

To the readers who pick up this book, thank you for your curiosity and interest in exploring the concept of beauty with me. I hope that the pages ahead provide you with insights, inspiration, and perhaps even a new perspective on the world around us.

With heartfelt appreciation,

Table of Contents:

Unveiling the Enigmatic Power of Beauty

The search for beauty is deeply ingrained in the human experience. Beauty permeates every aspect of our life, from the meticulously chosen works of art that grace our museums to the transient blossoms that fascinate our senses. Even still, it's difficult to sum up beauty in a single definition, even though its existence is evident.

Recognizing the diversity of beauty is the first step in understanding it. The Britannica Dictionary defines beauty as the "quality of being physically attractive" [1]. This is a concise definition. This definition, albeit succinct, only paints a partial picture of the situation. The Merriam-Webster dictionary has a broader definition of beauty that goes beyond the strictly physical, characterizing it as "the quality or aggregate of qualities in a person or thing that gives pleasure to the senses or pleasurably exalts the mind or spirit" [2]. This definition recognizes that beauty has the power to uplift our spirits, elicit wonder, and ignite joy in addition to its emotional and intellectual effects.

The fact that there are so many different conceptions of beauty emphasizes how complicated and dynamic it is.

Examining its historical development provides insight into the development of human communities. Every era has seen the growth and change of beauty ideals, reflecting the cultural values and beliefs of the time, from the magnificent sculptures of ancient Greece to the painstakingly designed gardens of the Edo period.

The study of beauty has significant consequences for comprehending human behavior, even beyond its historical significance. Several social and psychological research have demonstrated how profoundly beauty impacts our social connections. One key element influencing how our social lives are shaped is the idea of facial and body consonance, which refers to the harmonic balance of different aspects within the face and body [3]. According to research, those who are viewed as beautiful frequently enjoy greater success in both their personal and professional lives [4]. They are more likely to be seen as well-adjusted, wise, and trustworthy [4].

Moreover, research has shown a connection between career advancement and physical attractiveness. Beautiful people typically receive more positive performance reviews and are hired and promoted more frequently [4, 5]. Research indicates a troubling bias towards those perceived less attractive, demonstrating how attractiveness even affects the legal system. Less attractive people are more likely to be judged guilty and given harsher penalties, according to studies [6, 7, 8].

However, these observations should not be interpreted as endorsing a single, limited definition of beauty. Instead, they act as a sobering reminder of the societal expectations and unconscious prejudices that have the power to influence our thoughts and actions. We can move closer to a more inclusive and fair conception of beauty by recognizing the power dynamics at work and aggressively combating these prejudices.

Although the social and psychological effects of beauty are indisputable, it's important to understand that there are other routes to pleasure without pursuing external beauty. Nahai highlights the alluring power of beauty in its association with a variety of favorable attributes, such as contentment, financial benefit, reliability, and self-assurance [9]. True pleasure and self-worth, however, shouldn't depend only on fulfilling social norms regarding physical attractiveness.

Rather, it's crucial to develop a more comprehensive

definition of beauty that includes inward attributes like kindness, compassion, and intellectual curiosity. Through valuing individuality and diversity, we may cultivate a community that appreciates the depth of the human experience that goes beyond appearances.

The quest to understand the mysterious power of beauty is a lifelong investigation that necessitates a critical analysis of its cultural significance, personal interpretations, and historical foundations. Comprehending the intricate interactions among these components enables us to maneuver through the subtleties of beauty with enhanced consciousness and empathy, ultimately cultivating a more comprehensive and significant interpretation of this intricate notion.

Chapter 2: Beauty in the Philosopher's Lens: Objective or Subjective?

Though beauty can be seen in many things, such as the breathtaking majesty of nature or the minute intricacies in a piece of art, its fundamental qualities have fascinated philosophers for ages. Within Western philosophy, one of the most enduring—and sometimes contentious—themes is beauty. The primary point in this discussion is whether beauty is subjective and shaped only by societal influences and personal preferences, or if it is objective and exists outside of individual perception?

Objective beauty is the idea that things have beauty because of some underlying characteristics or principles. Plato's theory of forms, which contends that true beauty exists as an ideal, perfect form in the domain of ideas apart from the material world, is the source of this viewpoint. Humans experience things as beautiful because they believe that the world around them reflects this ideal beauty [1]. According to this perspective, beauty is something that exists regardless of personal preferences and that these intrinsic features influence our subjective impression of it.

On the other hand, the idea of subjective beauty contends that one's perception of beauty is wholly subjective and is influenced by one's emotional state, cultural background, and personal tastes. This viewpoint is in line with the beliefs of philosophers like David Hume, who maintained that individual preferences and experiences are the only factors that determine beauty [2]. He argued that an object's perceived beauty is entirely determined by our perception, which is influenced by our own experiences and the conditioning we receive from society. He did not believe that an object has any intrinsic beauty.

There are compelling reasons for both subjective and objective beauty, and the topic is still open. The universality of some aesthetic principles found across cultures and time periods is cited by proponents of objective beauty. For example, symmetry seems to be a universally appealing concept, as demonstrated by the admiration for symmetrical faces, buildings, and natural formations. This implies that there are universally applicable underlying rules that control beauty.

Moreover, proponents of objective beauty contend that there should be objective standards for evaluating beauty. They cite well-established aesthetic concepts like proportion, balance, and composition as signs of an artwork's intrinsic aesthetic worth. They contend that these ideas serve as a guide for artists, influencing both the production and appreciation of beautiful works and illuminating an objective side of beauty.

Subjective beauty proponents respond that convergent evolution is responsible for the seeming universality of some aesthetic ideas. Cultural influences and social standards can cause comparable conceptions of beauty to emerge throughout nations, much as natural selection can lead to similar qualities arising in distinct species. They contend that rather than being an innate principle, the appreciation of symmetry, for example, may be a learnt habit influenced by cultural preferences.

They also highlight the relativity of beauty standards that are observed in various historical eras and cultural contexts. What is regarded as attractive in one culture may not be in another. Comparably, standards of beauty can shift significantly throughout time, as seen by the development of fashion trends and the historical representation of ideal beauty in art. The existence of absolute, objective standards for beauty is called into question by this variety.

The nature vs. nurture controversy regarding beauty transcends philosophical boundaries and touches on psychology. Evolutionary psychology argues that our natural preferences may influence how we see beauty. This argument holds that certain traits, such symmetry in the face and clear skin, are indicators of excellent health and reproductive fitness, and that our ancestors evolved to associate these features unconsciously with beauty.

On the other hand, social psychology highlights how our conceptions of beauty are shaped by cultural conditioning . Our perception and appreciation of beauty are shaped by the images and messages that are continuously presented to us by the media, social conventions, and society expectations. These outside factors have the power to suppress any intrinsic preferences and cause the internalization of culturally defined beauty standards.

In conclusion, there is still no simple way to resolve the difficult question of whether beauty is subjective or objective. Both sides of the debate can make valid points, highlighting the importance of personal and societal factors or arguing for the existence of innate principles, but the truth may fall somewhere in the middle. Perhaps beauty is a complicated interaction of innate human tendencies, societal training, and personal experiences rather than something that is strictly objective or subjective. To appreciate beauty's complexity and promote a more inclusive and nuanced understanding of this timeless human experience, it is essential to comprehend the complex interplay between internal and external influences.

Chapter 3: Unveiling the Biological Canvas of Beauty: Exploring Physical Attributes

Beyond the fields of philosophy and aesthetics, human obsession with beauty is deeply ingrained in our DNA. A increasing amount of studies indicates that our innate biological constitution may play a role in our ability to discriminate between what is deemed "attractive" and what is not, in addition to cultural influences and personal preferences.

Numerous physical attributes have been recognized as possibly influencing how attractive someone is seen. This chapter explores these characteristics in detail, looking at both their biological foundation and the current controversy over their universal appeal.

1. **Facial Averageness:** According to the theory of facial averageness, more attractive faces typically resemble the average of a population's faces [1]. This effect implies that characteristics that depart less from the average may be more appealing to human brains, possibly signaling

improved health and genetic diversity [2]. A face that is deemed more appealing than any of the individual faces utilized in the average is frequently produced by averaging many faces, according to studies [3]. It's crucial to remember that face averageness is not a hard and fast rule, and that assessments of attractiveness can be greatly influenced by a variety of other characteristics.

2. Symmetry: Many historical eras and civilizations have long equated beauty with symmetry. Studies indicate that symmetrical faces are frequently regarded as more appealing [4]. There may be an evolutionary connection between symmetry and fitness and health. Asymmetry in facial characteristics may occasionally be a sign of underlying medical conditions or developmental disorders, and people may have unintentionally come to associate symmetry with health and the ability to procreate [5]. It's important to keep in mind that imperfect symmetry is not always present in nature and that some variations can still be deemed beautiful.

3. Skin Homogeneity: Smooth, clear skin is frequently connected to young appearance and health, which are attributes that have historically been connected to beauty. Research indicates that people find more beautiful people who have less wrinkles, blemishes, and uneven skin tone [6]. There may be an evolutionary benefit to selecting partners with healthy skin, as there is a correlation between strong immunity and good skin [7]. But it's crucial to recognize the variety of skin tones and how cultural norms shape ideas about skin "homogeneity."

4. Sexual Dimorphism: The morphological distinctions between males and females of the same species are referred to as sexual dimorphism. In humans, this shows up as traits like wider hips, bigger breasts, and fuller lips in women, and wider shoulders, wider jaws, and more facial hair in men [8]. These characteristics are frequently linked to attractiveness within their respective genders, which may indicate an evolutionary connection to successful reproduction and the capacity to conform to gender norms [9]. Nonetheless, it's critical to recognize how gender identities are changing and how society views the physical attributes of attractiveness.

The Evolving Narrative:

Our knowledge of these ostensibly universal traits is always changing. Even if research points to possible biological foundations, it's important to understand the limitations of these conclusions. It is impossible to ignore the impact of personal experiences, cultural conventions, and individual preferences. Furthermore, the idea of "beauty standards" is not universal, and different cultures and ethnic groups may have quite different ideas about what constitutes attractiveness. Moreover, the idea of a single, universal standard of beauty is called into question by the public's rising awareness of diversity and inclusivity.

Beyond the Biology:

It's critical to stress that physical appearance is only one component of the wide range of qualities that make someone attractive. Perceptions can be greatly influenced by traits such as intelligence, humor, shared values, personality, and shared ideals. Recognizing the interaction between a person's choices, cultural influences, and biological predispositions is necessary for a fully holistic knowledge of beauty. Going forward, encouraging a more diverse and equal society requires embracing beauty in all of its forms, recognizing individuality, and questioning strict beauty standards.

Chapter 4: The Quest for a Measure: Demystifying Attempts to Quantify Beauty

Humanity has struggled with the illusive idea of beauty throughout history, constantly trying to identify, comprehend, and even measure this complex sensation. This chapter explores the historical pursuit of quantifying beauty, looking at different approaches and considering their shortcomings.

The Golden Ratio and its Legacy:

Ancient Greece made one of the first recorded attempts to measure beauty. The golden ratio is a mathematical formula also referred to as the divine proportion, and it is credited to the artist Phidias (490–430 BCE). This ratio, which is represented as $(1 + \sqrt{5})/2$, suggests a certain ratio between two line segments that is meant to represent ideal aesthetic balance.

The golden ratio has been a staple of art and aesthetics for ages, even though its historical origins are still a mystery. The golden ratio functioned as a compass for artists striving to attain harmony and beauty in their creations, from the Parthenon's architectural marvels to the elaborate designs of the Renaissance.

The golden ratio is not universally accepted as a measure of beauty, though. Its application, according to critics, frequently entails subjective interpretations and selective measures, resulting in contradictions and a dearth of scientific data to back up its all-encompassing appeal.

Beyond the Golden Ratio: Modern Attempts at Quantification:

The quest to measure beauty has persisted since antiquity and is still going strong now. In an effort to provide scientific reasons for what people find attractive, modern academics have measured facial beauty using a variety of instruments and methods.

A popular method makes use of averaging techniques . A composite face depicting "average" traits is what researchers want to achieve by averaging the facial features of people within a population. According to studies, people frequently find these average looks to be more appealing than any one face in the sample [1]. This result is consistent with facial averageness theory and points to a possible biological explanation for our inclination toward characteristics that are more like the average of the population.

An alternative method for evaluating face features makes use of anthropometric measurements . Researchers assess the separations between the nose, lips, and eyes, among other locations on the face. The established ratios or ideal proportions thought to contribute to facial attractiveness are then compared to these measurements [2]. This method has drawbacks, too, since it only considers quantifiable features and ignores the dynamic interaction between distinct features and their combined aesthetic impact.

Furthermore, the emergence of computerized facial recognition technology has offered new avenues for quantifying beauty. These systems use pre-programmed algorithms to analyze facial features and assign scores. Although some advocates claim that these technologies provide objective measurements, questions still need to be answered about possible biases and culturally particular preferences ingrained in their algorithms.

The Limitations of Quantification:

It is important to acknowledge the inherent limitations of attempts to measure beauty, even in spite of continued efforts in this direction. Beyond only quantifiable characteristics, there are many other aspects that influence the complicated and subjective perception of beauty. Our view of beauty can be greatly influenced by a variety of factors, including personal tastes, historical events, cultural influences, and even emotional states.

Furthermore, there are ethical issues with measuring beauty. Individuals who do not fit into these specific classifications run the risk of being marginalized and excluded if we establish and promote unique, measurable norms. Furthermore, the quest of quantitative beauty may exacerbate social pressures and inflated expectations, which could have a detrimental impact on one's sense of self-worth and body image.

Beyond the Numbers: A Holistic Perspective on Beauty:

Though the quest for quantification provides fascinating

insights into the science of facial attractiveness, it's important to keep in mind that beauty is more than just a number. As we move forward, we must adopt a more comprehensive view of beauty, taking into account the intricate interactions between a person's own preferences, cultural influences, and biological predispositions.

Furthermore, the development of a culture in which beauty is not quantified but rather accepted in its complex and ever-changing nature requires a movement toward an appreciation of the varied tapestry of human beauty, honoring distinctive qualities, and promoting inclusivity.

Chapter 5: A Tapestry Through Time: Evolving Beauty Standards Across Eras

Despite appearing to be universal, the definition of beauty is dynamic. Its expression, perception, and interpretation have fascinatingly changed over time, mirroring the social mores, artistic trends, and cultural values of each period. This chapter explores the fascinating journey of beauty through several eras, demonstrating how it is always changing.

Prehistoric Era: Enigmatic Beginnings:

We start our investigation in the prehistoric past, when the meaning of beauty standards is lost in the mists of time. An enigmatic symbol of this era is the famous Venus of Willendorf , a voluptuous female figurine from 25,000–30,000 BCE. Though opinions on its meaning and purpose differ, some believe it to be a fertility emblem, implying an early correlation between attractiveness and traits associated with reproduction [1].

Ancient Civilizations: Diverse Ideals:

As time goes on, various and distinctive criteria of beauty are revealed by ancient civilizations all across the world. Slender bodies with dark features, narrow hips, and high waists were highly regarded as the embodiment of beauty in Ancient Egypt [2]. Women accentuated their eyes and added a sense of mystery by donning heavy eye makeup, especially eyeliner.

Ancient Greece , in sharp contrast, placed a premium on physical prowess and agility. Goddesses such as Aphrodite and Athena were depicted in sculpture with strong bodies, harmonious faces, and proportions that were harmonized [3]. The groundwork for Western European beauty standards for decades to come was formed by this idealization of physical perfection.

Medieval Europe: Shifting Focus:

When the Middle Ages arrived in Europe, the emphasis shifted to religious conceptions of beauty. Piety, inner beauty, and a pale complexion, which denoted aristocracy, were frequently valued above only physical characteristics [4]. Dressing modestly and covering their hair, women reflected the social and religious norms of the day.

The Renaissance: A Rebirth of Ideals:

A resurgence of interest in classical Greek and Roman ideas arose with the   Renaissance . In their works, sculptors and artists such as Michelangelo and Botticelli brought back to life the ancient emphasis on symmetry, proportion, and idealized physical perfection [5]. Around this time, there was also a resurgence of interest in the idealized shapes and sensuous expressions that characterize human beauty, regardless of gender.

The Age of Enlightenment and the Rise of Individualism:

Diverse perspectives on beauty and an increasing emphasis on personal expression were introduced throughout the   Age of Enlightenment . Although there was still a common norm of refinement and elegance, beauty shifted to become more individualized and reflect particular tastes and styles [6]. During this time, fashion trends and cosmetics that catered to personal preferences also emerged.

The Modern Era: A Globalized Landscape:

The way that people view beauty has changed significantly in the 20th and 21st centuries. The world is now more interconnected due to globalization, which has exposed people to a variety of cultural customs and beauty standards. Due to the challenge to conventional, rigid notions of beauty, openness and diversity have gained more acceptance .

The media landscape of today greatly shapes and influences ideals of beauty. Increased media diversity and portrayal of many ethnicities, body sizes, and genders are striving for a more inclusive and complex understanding of beauty, even while worries about unrealistic representations and the promotion of restricted ideals still exist [7].

Beyond the Surface: Embracing Inner Beauty:

Throughout history, physical appearance has frequently been the primary emphasis of the desire of beauty. But inner beauty is a crucial component of beauty that is sometimes disregarded. This includes character traits like integrity, generosity, and intelligence. Understanding the significance of inner beauty promotes a more comprehensive interpretation of the idea and inspires us to value people for who they really are, beyond appearances.

A Continuing Legacy:

Today's standards of beauty are continually developing as a result of the ever-changing social and cultural environments. The historical background of beauty standards must be understood, as must its subjectivity and flexibility. We must work toward a future where beauty is defined by diversity, inclusivity, and an appreciation of both inner and outer aspects.

Chapter 6: A Tapestry of Beauty: Embracing Diversity Beyond Ethnicity

While symmetry and averageness are seen as largely universal qualities of beauty, different cultural and ethnic groups have distinct perspectives on beauty and diverse face traits. Only a few research works have examined this complex idea. This chapter explores the enthralling tapestry of beauty standards woven across various locations and civilizations, going beyond ethnic boundaries. It underscores the significance of cultivating cultural sensitivity and honoring the distinct manifestations of beauty that cut beyond racial boundaries.

Moving Beyond the Ethnic Lens: Exploring Regional Influences

Strictly focusing on ethnicity may restrict our perception of what constitutes beauty. Perceptions of beauty are significantly shaped by regional and cultural influences , which extend beyond ethnic boundaries. A deeper and more complex understanding of the worldwide fabric of beauty can be attained by investigating these various influences.

Ancient Civilizations and Evolving Ideals:

The fascinating relationship between   cultural beliefs, creative manifestations, and beauty standards   can be revealed by delving into history. Ancient societies with particular notions of beauty, such as the Greeks, Romans, and Egyptians, frequently mirrored these goals in their art and architecture. Even though these values were situated inside their particular cultures, they frequently cut over racial boundaries. For instance, both Egyptian and non-Egyptian painters in the area were impacted by the Egyptian ideal of proportion and symmetry .

Religious Influences and Diverse Expressions:

Perceptions of beauty are also greatly influenced by religion   and   spirituality.   Certain   qualities   or characteristics may be emphasized by different religions as symbols of purity, piety, or divine favor. For example, long, flowing hair may be linked with beauty in some cultures   because   of   its   religious   significance.

Understanding these various perspectives brings to reveal the intricate relationship that exists between faith and beauty in all civilizations.

Social and Economic Factors:

Beauty standards are also influenced by socioeconomic factors, including access to resources, wealth, and status. There has always been a relationship between beauty and social standing since some traits or behaviors have been connected to the upper class. Even though there may be issues with this association, it's important to understand its cultural and historical background within each group.

The Evolving Landscape of Beauty:

Beauty standards are dynamic and ever-evolving , shaped by a number of forces such as social movements, globalization, and technological breakthroughs. Cross-cultural influences are reshaping beauty standards as civilizations get more interconnected, creating a more inclusive and diversified landscape .

Beyond Physical Attributes: Embracing Inner Beauty

While perceptions of beauty are influenced by outward appearance, inner beauty is equally important. Certain cultures may place a greater emphasis on qualities like kindness, strength, and wisdom than others. concept and valuing the various ways that inner beauty manifests itself in different cultural contexts promotes a more holistic concept of beauty .

Challenging Harmful Practices and Promoting Inclusivity:

It's vital to consider the possible effects of beauty standards. Extreme bodily alteration or skin bleaching are two examples of activities that can be damaging and maintain unequal power dynamics . Creating a more fair and empowered landscape of beauty requires promoting diversity and opposing destructive behaviors.

Embracing Diversity: Celebrating Individuality

In the end, embracing individuality and celebrating diversity is the path to true beauty. It's important to acknowledge and value the distinctive qualities, cultural influences, and life experiences that make each person beautiful in their own right. This change in viewpoint encourages a more inclusive and joyous environment for all, pushing us beyond restrictive standards.

The Power of Storytelling:

A potent method for promoting cultural sensitivity and recognizing various standards of beauty is storytelling. We learn more about people's unique viewpoints and experiences related to beauty by hearing their stories from people from a variety of cultures and backgrounds. This can be accomplished by dispelling negative stereotypes and fostering empathy via media like social media, books, and movies.

A World Beyond Borders:

We can create a society where beauty is embraced in all its many expressions by eschewing the confines of ethnicity and embracing the complex tapestry of regional, cultural, and personal influences. This change in viewpoint enables us to see past constrictive definitions and appreciate the richness and complexity of what makes each person special and lovely.

Conclusion: Celebrating the Tapestry of Human Beauty

We may fully comprehend the fascinating tapestry of human beauty, woven from individual experiences, cultural influences, and the distinctive expressions of inner and exterior beauty, as we advance toward a world that honors diversity and promotes cultural sensitivity.

Chapter 7: The Body Positive Movement: Exploring Body Image, Acceptance, and Diversity

Following strict and frequently unachievable beauty standards, the Body Positive Movement has become a potent movement that questions social conventions and encourages acceptance and love for oneself. This chapter explores the fundamental ideas of the movement, how it affects people on an individual and societal level, and how it continues to strive for a more inclusive and varied concept of beauty.

Understanding Body Image: The Root of Self-Perception

The term body image describes how we view and feel about our own physical attributes. Personal experiences, societal expectations, and media portrayals all play a complex role in shaping our thoughts, feelings, and beliefs about our bodies. Negative body image, which is frequently influenced by unattainable beauty standards, can cause severe mental and emotional distress, such as low self-esteem, anxiety, and depression.

The Genesis of the Body Positive Movement:

Challenging the dominant beauty standard and advancing a more inclusive image of beauty, the Body Positive Movement was born out of feminist activism and fat acceptance efforts in the 1990s. The movement highlights

Body acceptance: Embracing and appreciating one's body, regardless of size, shape, or appearance.

Self-love: Cultivating positive self-regard and self-worth, independent of external validation.

Challenging beauty standards: De-constructing unrealistic and harmful beauty ideals that exclude diverse body types and ethnicities.

Diversity and inclusion: Celebrating the unique physical attributes and characteristics that make each individual beautiful.

The Ripple Effect: Impacting Individuals and Society

The Body Positive Movement has had a profound effect on people's lives as well as society overall. Here are a few salient features of its impact:

Empowering individuals: The movement provides tools and resources to help individuals develop positive body image, challenge negative self-talk, and cultivate self-compassion.

Promoting self-acceptance: By normalizing diverse body types and challenging societal expectations, the movement encourages individuals to embrace their unique appearances and appreciate their bodies for their functionality and strength.

Influencing media representation: The movement has sparked changes in the media, supporting body-positive messaging, increasing diversity in actors and models, and opposing the glamorization of unattainable beauty standards.

Starting social conversations : The Body Positive Movement has sparked important dialogues on the detrimental effects of unattainable beauty standards on mental health, self-esteem, and body image. These dialogues are leading the way towards a society that is more accepting and inclusive.

Challenges and Opportunities: Moving Towards Inclusivity

Notwithstanding its beneficial effects, the Body Positive Movement has several drawbacks:

Internalized negativity: Deeply ingrained societal expectations and negative narratives often lead to internalized negativity, making it difficult for individuals to fully embrace self-acceptance.

Limited reach: The movement's message might not always reach marginalized communities or individuals with diverse body types beyond the "body positive" spectrum, requiring continuous efforts towards inclusivity.

Commodification: The movement's main message may be weakened if "body positivity" becomes more commercialized as a result of its growing popularity.

However, the Body Positive Movement presents exciting opportunities:

Creating a more inclusive beauty industry: The movement can work to create a more inclusive beauty business that accommodates a greater range of body shapes and races by promoting varied representation in the media and fashion.

Promoting mental health awareness : By bringing attention to the connection between mental health and body image, the movement can foster candid discussions about mental health issues and provide options for those in need of help.

Encouraging education and dialogue: The movement may dispel stereotypes, inform people of the negative effects of unattainable beauty standards, and advance body literacy in a variety of areas by launching educational programs and encouraging candid conversation.

The Power of Authenticity: Embracing Your Story

In the end, people are empowered by the Body Positive Movement to reclaim their narratives and celebrate their unique stories . People can develop a good body image and help create a world where beauty is defined by more than just surface criteria by accepting individuality, practicing self-compassion, and questioning social norms.

Stories that Inspire:

Narrating personal tales of conquering negative body image and accepting oneself can be a potent means of promoting compassion and understanding. Through establishing secure environments where people may open up about their experiences, the Body Positive Movement enables people to connect with one another and receive support.

Looking Forward: A World of Diverse Beauty

The goal of the Body Positive Movement is to redefine beauty and create a society in which each individual is empowered to accept and value their own unique self. Together, we can challenge harmful habits, celebrate individuality, encourage good body image, and enable everyone to feel the joy of self-acceptance. Together, we can build a society that values individuality and positive body image.

Chapter 8: The Globalization of Beauty: A Tapestry of Diversity and Homogenization

Every culture has a complex definition of beauty, yet it has never remained static. Though previous ideas of beauty may have differed greatly across geographic boundaries, the idea of distinct, isolated beauty standards is being challenged by the growing interconnectedness of the world. The complexities of the globalization of beauty are examined in this chapter, along with the possibility of homogenization and the continuous struggle for diversity and inclusivity .

Melting Borders and Shifting Perceptions:

There are several reasons for the blurring of cultural boundaries that globalization has enabled, including:

Global migration patterns and easier travel: People's perspectives of beauty are expanded as a result of exposure to a wider range of cultural norms and aesthetics.

Media and technology: The pervasiveness of media, especially social media, makes it possible for international beauty trends and aesthetics to be widely disseminated and to influence people all over the world.

Economic factors: The emergence of globalized markets and multinational firms can bring Western standards of beauty to previously untapped countries, thereby influencing consumer tastes and possibly forming local beauty standards.

The Rise of "Global Beauty": A Homogenizing Force?

The concept of "global beauty" frequently prompts worries about the possibility of cultural homogenization in which a dominating, frequently Western-centric ideal may eclipse a variety of beauty standards. This might be:

Problematic: It may cause people who don't fit the mainstream standard to be marginalized ,which could exacerbate feelings of inadequacy and insecurity, especially in young people who are exposed to idealized representations on social media.

Restricted: It ignores the diverse range of cultural influences and individual manifestations of beauty that exist worldwide, as well as the historical and social background that forms various conceptions of beauty.

Examining the Homogenizing Effect:

There are several ways in which globalization has an impact:

Western beauty norms being promoted in non-Western markets: Advertising campaigns that predominantly feature Western models and beauty standards may lead to the impression that these standards are accepted worldwide, which may engender feelings of inferiority in those who don't fit the mold.

The emergence of international beauty pageants: Although these venues seek to honor beauty on a worldwide scale, there are worries that they might unintentionally encourage a limited notion of beauty, frequently endorsing attributes that are Eurocentric.

The urge to conform: Trends in social media and continuous exposure to idealized pictures can put young people under pressure to meet a certain, frequently unachievable standard of beauty.

Celebrating Diversity: Embracing the Tapestry of Beauty

Globalization has the tendency to homogenize people, yet there are countervailing forces that support cultural sensitivity and celebrate diversity:

The development of social justice movements : Calls for racial and ethnic inclusivity, as well as groups like Body Positive, question limited definitions of beauty and encourage acceptance and appreciation of a variety of body shapes, ethnic traits, and cultural expressions of beauty.

Multicultural media representation: As the need for varied representation in media and entertainment grows, people of different racial and ethnic backgrounds, as well as different body types, are being included. This is showcasing a wider range of beauty and encouraging respect for various aesthetic ideals.

Local ownership and innovation: As local beauty trends and brands that cater to particular cultural tastes arise, diversity is allowed to continue and distinctive expressions of beauty within various cultural settings are celebrated.

Examples of Embracing Diversity:

The emergence of Korean beauty trends: The growing respect for varied beauty practices and aesthetics beyond Western-centric standards is demonstrated by the widespread appeal of Korean skincare regimens and beauty products.

The celebration of indigenous beauty: Movements within different indigenous communities are contesting the prevailing narratives about beauty while reclaiming and honoring their traditional cultural practices and ideals of beauty. This promotes cultural pride.

Inclusive representation in fashion: A more inclusive and representative representation of beauty in the industry is being facilitated by the growing number of fashion designers and brands including various models and aesthetics into their campaigns and catwalk shows.

The Potential Downsides of Celebrating Diversity:

Although it's good to celebrate diversity in beauty, there are certain drawbacks that should be considered as well:

Tokenism: It can be detrimental to unintentionally include people from different backgrounds without providing authentic representation or acknowledging their distinct cultural context.

Commodification of diversity: It can be insulting and detrimental to the movement's basic ideals to use diversity just for commercial gain, without addressing the underlying problems of equity and representation.

The Future of Beauty: Embracing a Multifaceted Landscape

It is conceivable that beauty will have many facets in the future, which include:

Acknowledgment of differing beauty standards: Acknowledging and valuing the various ways that different cultures define beauty while advancing tolerance and acceptance.

Globalization's ongoing influence: Global trends will probably continue to shape how people view beauty, but they'll probably do so with a greater emphasis on personal expression and cultural context.

Evolving technology: New developments in technology could influence future standards of beauty by encouraging more customization and personalization in the beauty sector. This could consist of:

The application of artificial intelligence (AI):

Tools with AI capabilities could tailor product recommendations and beauty advice to each user's requirements and tastes.

Virtual reality (VR) and augmented reality (AR): These technologies could let people virtually try on clothes or attempt other looks before committing, encouraging educated decisions and customized experiences.

Conclusion: A Celebration of Individuality

Celebrating the unique manifestations of beauty found within each individual is the ultimate goal, despite the problems and opportunities presented by the globalization of beauty. It is imperative to embrace diversity, cultivate cultural sensitivity, and advance self-acceptance in order to establish a society in which all individuals are enabled to enjoy their individuality and relish in self-love.

We must work together to navigate this path towards a future of beauty that is more diverse and inclusive. People are able to accept cultural diversity, dispel negative prejudices, and value their distinctive qualities. Companies can support ethical marketing techniques, give priority to varied representation, and attend to the demands of each customer. When we work together, we can build a society where beauty transcends homogeneity and instead honors the diverse range of personal expressions and cultural influences that give each person their own special beauty.

Chapter 9: The Allure and Paradox of Social Media Influencers: Navigating the Evolving Landscape of Beauty

Social media has emerged as an unavoidable force in today's technologically advanced society, reshaping our views and impacting many facets of our life, including how we perceive and value beauty. Social media influencers are at the vanguard of this movement; these are people who use their online platforms to advertise goods, set trends, and eventually change the way we see and define beauty. In the constantly changing world of beauty, this chapter explores the complexities surrounding the role of social media influencers and their allure as well as potential pitfalls .

The Allure of Social Media Influencers and the Power of Perception:

Social media influencers are appealing because of their personal level audience connections. They portray themselves as approachable people, frequently sharing their daily schedules, cosmetic advice, and product suggestions. Its authenticity and accessibility help viewers relate to the show, especially younger audiences who might find traditional media characters less understandable. Furthermore, influencers frequently design their online personas to embody particular aesthetic ideals ,advancing particular standards of beauty and influencing people's perceptions of what is "attractive" or "desirable."

Exploring the Impact: Positive and Negative Influences

Social media influencers have a complex effect on how people perceive beauty, with both possible advantages and disadvantages:

Positive Influences:

Encouraging Inclusivity and Diversity: A growing number of influencers are defying limited notions of beauty by exhibiting a range of gender identities, races, and body types. For those who previously felt alienated from popular media and beauty standards, this portrayal can be uplifting.

Inspiring Experimentation and Self-Care: Numerous influencers provide their personal skincare routines, makeup techniques, and style advice, inspiring and motivating their audience to try out new beauty products.

Creating Connections and Building Communities: By engaging with their followers through interactive content, addressing shared issues, and promoting candid conversations on a range of beauty-related themes, influencers can establish a feeling of community and belonging.

Negative Influences:

Unrealistic Beauty Standards: Regrettably, a lot of influencers promote very carefully chosen and Photoshopped images , which reinforces unattainable and unrealistic beauty standards. Viewers may experience emotions of inadequacy, uncertainty, and discontent as a result, especially young people who are more vulnerable to the effects of social media.

Encouraging Unhealthy Behaviors: Certain influencers may purposefully or inadvertently encourage dangerous behaviors in an effort to meet or uphold particular ideals of beauty. This could involve using filters excessively, encouraging unattainable physical changes, or supporting unhealthful exercise regimens or restrictive diets.

The Need to Fit in: There may be pressure to follow particular trends and beauty standards when one is constantly exposed to carefully manicured online personas. This can have a detrimental effect on one's sense of self-worth, cause social comparison anxiety, and make it more difficult for people to accept their individuality and see the beauty within.

Beyond the Superficial: Unveiling the Curated Reality

It's important to keep in mind that social media influencers' online presence frequently represents a well manicured reality . Photos are extensively manipulated, a lot of filters are used, and only some facets of people's lives are shown. It is essential to acknowledge the constructed nature of online personas in order to lessen the detrimental effects of unattainable beauty standards.

Strategies for Navigating the Influencer Landscape:

Several tactics can be used to manage the convoluted and frequently contradictory world of social media influencers and their impact on the perception of beauty:

Cultivate a Critical Lens: View online content critically by challenging the veracity of excessively Photoshopped photos and acknowledging how influencers' narratives are shaped by marketing and brand alliances.

Embrace Diversity: Look for and follow influencers who embody a range of races, body shapes, and standards of beauty. Your perception of beauty may change as a result of this exposure, and the idea of a single, universal standard may be questioned.

Acceptance of Oneself: Place more emphasis on appreciating your own special traits and developing self-acceptance based on internal attributes and ideals than on seeking approval from others or fitting in with fictitious internet representations.

Reduce Social Media Use: Set aside time for activities that promote self-love and an appreciation of your unique attractiveness, and keep an eye on how much time you spend on social media.

The Future of Social Media Influencers and the Evolving Landscape:

Social media's environment and how it affects how people view beauty are always changing. New platforms and tools will appear as technology develops, possibly further obfuscating the distinctions between real life and virtual identities. However, in the end, it will need collaboration between people, brands, and platforms to develop a positive and inclusive concept of beauty:

People: putting self-acceptance first, accepting varied representations, and engaging in critical thought.

Brands: refraining from upholding unattainable beauty standards, supporting ethical marketing techniques, and placing a high value on diversity and inclusivity in partnerships with influencers.

Platforms: Enacting laws to prevent over-editing of images and encouraging openness about sponsored content.

Chapter 10: Beauty Unbound: A Celebration of Self-Discovery and Acceptance

Our investigation into beauty has led us on an incredible voyage, revealing its deep impact on our existence. We have seen the continuing strength of this complex idea from the depths of ancient history, when beauty was cherished in mythology and art, to the ever-changing modern world, saturated with varied perspectives and digital influences. We have explored the nuances of defining beauty, appreciating its cultural diversity, and overcoming obstacles brought on by society norms and media representations during this voyage.

It is becoming more and more obvious that beauty cannot be reduced to a single concept or defined by a set of strict standards as we stand on the edge of the future. As a entity with several facets and dynamics , it is molded by the intricate interaction of personal experiences, cultural influences, and hereditary traits . This knowledge opens the door to a more powerful and inclusive view of beauty, one that values diversity and recognizes the individuality of every person.

Embracing the Tapestry of Beauty:

The appreciation of beauty's inherent diversity is at the core of an interpretation of beauty that is really inclusive and transformational. This includes recognizing and respecting:

  The diversity of cultural manifestations: Every culture has its own ideas about beauty that are shaped by its social values, history, and customs. Accepting this variability enables us to see the rich tapestry of human beauty and transcend rigid norms. We start to perceive beauty not as an isolated thing but rather as a colorful mosaic made up of many unique expressions and cultural subtleties.

  The range of distinct expressions: Every person has distinct physical traits and personal preferences that add to their innate beauty. Giving up on a one-size-fits-all strategy enables us to see and honor unique beauty in all of its manifestations. We acknowledge that beauty extends beyond physical characteristics to include the distinct array of character traits, abilities, and life events that mold each person.

  The beauty that transcends the material: Beauty extends beyond appearances and includes inner qualities such as kindness, compassion, fortitude, and intellectual curiosity. By acknowledging and valuing these intrinsic attributes, we can develop a more complete perception of beauty . It inspires us to see past outward manifestations and uncover the genuine nature of a person's nature and soul.

Shifting the Focus: Beyond Superficiality:

The quest for a more profound and significant relationship with beauty demands a change in perspective, from superficiality to substance . This voyage entails:

Moving past irrational expectations: It becomes imperative to acknowledge and confront the unattainable and frequently detrimental ideals of beauty that are propagated by the media and social influences. This entails encouraging critical thinking abilities, challenging the veracity of carefully chosen internet personas, and aggressively advancing ideas of body positivity and self-acceptance. We can escape the vicious cycle of uneasiness and comparison by confronting unreasonable expectations and embracing our true selves.

Developing an acceptance of oneself: Accepting ourselves as we are is the first step toward realizing our own attractiveness. This entails developing self-love and compassion, accepting our unique qualities, and recognizing our strengths and shortcomings. Through practicing self-acceptance, we discover intrinsic value that goes beyond approval from others and learn to value ourselves for who we really are, flaws and all.

Putting inner beauty first: Our total perception of beauty is greatly influenced by developing a positive self-image and nurturing our inner attributes. This entails honing our skills, learning new things, and cultivating compassion and goodwill. By putting our attention on developing our inner selves, we enhance our general wellbeing and foster an inner beauty.

A Shared Responsibility: Cultivating an Inclusive Future:

Creating a world where beauty transcends superficiality and embraces diversity requires a collective effort :

Individuals: We may make a difference by actively advocating inclusivity in private settings, questioning biased representations, developing self-acceptance and acceptance in ourselves and others, and engaging in critical thinking when consuming media.

Influencers and media: Influencers and the media both have a big part to play in supporting ethical marketing techniques, showing off a variety of portrayals of beauty, and avoiding promoting unattainable standards. They may help create a media environment that is more accepting and uplifting by embracing diversity and advancing positive themes.

Schools and colleges: By encouraging critical thinking abilities, encouraging conversations on body image and self-acceptance, celebrating a variety of cultural expressions and beliefs, and providing safe spaces for candid conversation, educational institutions may play a significant role in society. Giving people the right resources and information will enable them to make sense of the complicated issues surrounding beauty and develop positive self-images.

Policies and governments: Putting in place moral guidelines for marketing and advertising campaigns, encouraging media literacy programs, and hosting public forums on mental health and beauty standards can all help society move toward a more accepting and empowering definition of beauty.

Embracing the Journey of Self-Discovery:

Ultimately, the quest for beauty is not about arriving at a fixed destination

www.ingramcontent.com/pod-product-compliance
Lightning Source LLC
Chambersburg PA
CBHW072156020426
42334CB00018B/2035